"I intend to write a rave about *The Art of Procrastination* just as soon as I've cleared my desk this afternoon—or at least by first thing tomorrow—because reading this straight-talking, badly needed book has changed my life."

—Bruce McCall, writer and illustrator for *The New Yorker*

"There are lessons both deep and funny to be found in our capacity to put things off, and Perry is the ideal guide—a writer of superlative wisdom and wit. Forget whatever you were supposed to do next, and read this book."

—Mark Kingwell, PhD, coauthor of *The Idler's Glossary*

"*The Art of Procrastination* rings startlingly true. Perry reconstructs the inner dialogue of the procrastinator with a droll, lighthearted style that has inspired me to try his strategies (alarm clocks, self-deceptions, and self-forgiveness)."

—Patrick Byrne, CEO, Overstock.com

THE ART

of

PROCRASTINATION

A GUIDE TO EFFECTIVE
DAWDLING, LOLLYGAGGING
AND POSTPONING

JOHN PERRY

WORKMAN PUBLISHING
NEW YORK

Library of Congress Cataloging-in-Publication Data is available.

ISBN 978-0-7611-7167-6

Design by Sarah Smith

Workman books are available at special discounts when purchased in bulk
for premiums and sales promotions as well as for fund-raising or educational
use. Special editions or book excerpts can also be created to specification.
For details, contact the Special Sales Director at the address below, or send
an email to specialmarkets@workman.com.

Workman Publishing Company, Inc.
225 Varick Street
New York, NY 10014-4381

workman.com

Printed in the United States of America
First printing August 2012

10 9 8 7 6 5 4 3 2 1

For Frenchie
Who is very patient (sometimes)

"Never put off until tomorrow what you can do the day after tomorrow."

—MARK TWAIN

ACKNOWLEDGMENTS

Two late friends—the great writer Tony Burciaga and Bob Beyers, also a fine writer and for a long time the head of the Stanford News Service—were the first to suggest that I should try to publish the essay "Structured Procrastination." Beyers somehow convinced *The Chronicle of Higher Education* to do so in 1996. Marc Abrahams, the genius behind the *Annals of Improbable Research*, reprinted it in that journal soon after. Years later, in 2011, I was awarded another one of Abrahams's inventions, the Ig Nobel Prize for Literature. Deborah Wilkes of Hackett Publications, who has often suffered from my procrastinating, accepted the award for me at Harvard Ig Nobel awards ceremony, which I was unable to attend. Participating in this rather wild event required good humor and courage on her part, although I don't think she knew that when she agreed to do it. Between 1996 and 2011 Erin Perry, one of my granddaughters, grew up, learned all about Web pages, and created one for this essay and a couple of others. This generated a lot of interesting responses from readers. A number of my friends thought all of this material might make a small book, but I didn't take this suggestion seriously until it came from

Barney Karpfinger, now my agent, who had read about the Ig Nobel Prize. I'm very grateful to all of these folks, and to my editor, Margot Herrera, and her colleagues at Workman Publishing, who have been delightful to work with. My procrastination has been hard on my family—hardest of all on my lovely wife, Frenchie—but all have been good sports.

CONTENTS

INTRODUCTION
The Paradox of Procrastination

Humans are by nature rational animals. Our ability to reason is supposedly what sets us apart from other animals, so it seems we ought to be incredibly reasonable, basing each action on deliberation and doing the best possible thing according to those deliberations. Plato and Aristotle were so caught up in this ideal that they found a philosophical problem in our failure to live up to it: *akrasia*, the mystery of why people choose to do other than what they think is best for them to do.

This picture of humans as rational beings that base their actions on deliberations and calculations about what is best has stuck around since it was articulated in ancient times. The more mathematical social sciences, such as economics, are largely based on the conception of humans as rational animals that make choices on the basis of what action is most likely to promote their most important desires. This is rather odd, given that many of the other social sciences, including psychology and sociology, provide ample evidence that we don't work like that at all.

I really have nothing against rationality, or even doing what you think is best, or doing what is most likely to satisfy your desires. I have tried these strategies at various times, occasionally with good results. But I think the ideal of the rational agent is the source of lots of needless unhappiness. It's not the way many of us operate; it's certainly not the way I operate. And operating the way we do usually works just fine, and really isn't a reason to hang our heads in shame and despair.

My most prominent failing, in terms of this ideal, is procrastination. In 1995, while not working on some project I should have been working on, I began to feel rotten about myself. But then I noticed something. On the whole, I had a reputation as a person who got a lot done and made a reasonable contribution to Stanford University, where I worked, and to the discipline of philosophy, which is what I work on. A paradox. Rather than getting to work on my important projects, I began to think about this conundrum. I realized that I was what I call a *structured procrastinator*: a person who gets a lot done by not doing other things. I wrote the little essay that is the first chapter of this book and immediately began to feel better about myself.

This essay was subsequently published in *The Chronicle of Higher Education* and the satiric science magazine *Annals of Improbable Research,* and I posted it on my Stanford webpage. Now, I am a professional philosopher, strange as that may sound to most people. I've written scores of articles and half a dozen

books. These articles and books, in my humble opinion, are full of deep insights, profound wisdom, and
clever analyses, and they advance our understanding
of all sorts of interesting things—from free will to
personal identity to the nature of meaning. My parents are dead, so I may be the only one who thinks so
highly of my work in philosophy. But since I got into
Stanford by the back door, as a faculty member—for I
never would have been admitted as an undergraduate
or graduate student—my body of work has sufficed to
keep me employed as a philosophy teacher. So it must
not be utter drivel.

Be that as it may, nothing I have written has been
read by so many, been helpful to so many—at least by
their own testimony—and brightened as many days
as my little essay on structured procrastination. For
many years that article was the number one hit when
one googled *procrastination*. After I moved it from
my Stanford webpage to a private website (www.struc
turedprocrastination.com) so I could sell Structured
Procrastination T-shirts, it fell in the ranking and then

rose again, so now it's usually not too far below the *Wikipedia* article on procrastination. Each month I receive a dozen or so emails from readers. They are virtually all positive, and some say the essay has had considerable impact. Here's one example:

> Dear John,
>
> Your essay on structured procrastination just changed my life. Already I feel better about myself. I have accomplished thousands of tasks over the past few months, all the while feeling terrible about the fact that they weren't the really important ones that sat above them on the priority list. But now I begin to find the cumulonimbus clouds of guilt and shame above me are lifting. . . . Thank you.

My favorite email was from a woman who said that she had been a procrastinator all of her life. Being a procrastinator had made her miserable, she said, in large part because her brother was constantly critical of her for having this character flaw. Reading my essay, she said, allowed her to hold her head up and realize that she is a valuable human being who accomplishes a great deal, in spite of being a procrastinator. After reading it, she said, for the first time in her life, she had the courage to tell her brother to shut up and get lost. "By the way," she added, "I am seventy-two years old."

Over the years I have intended to add to the essay, although, characteristically, I kept putting it off. Gradually, from reading the emails I've received, introspecting, doing a lot of thinking and a little reading, I have come to realize that grasping the concept of structured procrastination is only the first step in a program that I think can help the large majority of procrastinators, as it has me. Oddly enough, once we realize that we are structured procrastinators, not only do we feel better about ourselves but we also actually improve somewhat in our ability to get things done, because, once the miasma of guilt and despair clears, we have a better understanding of what keeps us from doing those things.

So this book presents a sort of philosophical self-help program for depressed procrastinators. Truth be told, calling it a program is a bit generous. It starts out with a couple of helpful steps that procrastinators can take. After that it offers up some ideas, anecdotes, and suggestions that might be helpful. I also say a bit about the organizational problems that beleaguer many procrastinators.

Not all people are procrastinators, and not all procrastinators will be helped by recognizing the strategy of structured procrastination, because procrastination is sometimes a manifestation of deeper problems that require more therapy than lighthearted philosophy can provide. Still, if my email in-box is any guide, many people will find themselves in these pages and as a result will feel better about themselves. Not to mention the added bonus that they'll encounter some rather nice concepts and words to apply to themselves, such as *akrasia*, *horizontal organization*, *task triage*, and *right-parenthesis deficit disorder*. And some of these people may even get more done.

CHAPTER ONE

Structured Procrastination

I have been intending to write this essay for months. Why am I finally doing it? Because I finally found some uncommitted time? Wrong. I have papers to grade, textbook orders to fill out, a National Science Foundation proposal to referee, and dissertation drafts to read. I am working on this essay as a way of not doing all of those things. This is the essence of what I call *structured procrastination*, an amazing strategy I have discovered that converts procrastinators into effective human beings, respected and admired for all that they accomplish and the good use they make of time.

(Or at any rate I rediscovered it. In 1930 Robert Benchley wrote a column for the *Chicago Tribune* titled "How to Get Things Done," in which he stated that "anyone can do any amount of work, provided it isn't the work he is *supposed* to be doing at that moment." As that quotation shows, Benchley saw the fundamental principle—and I assume other profound thinkers who were structured procrastinators like he was have noticed the same thing. Someday I'll do some further research.)

All procrastinators put off things they have to do. Structured procrastination is the art of making this negative trait work for you. The key idea is that procrastinating does not mean doing absolutely nothing. Procrastinators seldom do absolutely nothing; they do marginally useful things, such as gardening or sharpening pencils or making a diagram of how they will reorganize their files when they get around to it.

Why does the procrastinator do these things? Because they are a way of not doing something more important. If all the procrastinator had left to do was to sharpen some pencils, no force on earth could get him to do it. The procrastinator can be motivated to do difficult, timely, and important tasks, however, as long as these tasks are a way of not doing something more important.

Structured procrastination means shaping the structure of the tasks one has to do in a way that exploits this fact. In your mind, or perhaps even written down somewhere, you have a list of things you want to accomplish, ordered by importance. You might even call this your priority list. Tasks that seem most urgent and important are on top. But there are also worthwhile tasks to perform lower down on the list. Doing these tasks becomes a way of not doing the things higher up on the list. With this sort of appropriate task structure the procrastinator becomes a useful citizen. Indeed, the procrastinator can even acquire, as I have, a reputation for getting a lot done.

The most perfect situation for structured procrastination that I ever had was when my wife and I served as resident fellows in Soto House, a Stanford dormitory. In the evening, faced with papers to grade, lectures to prepare, committee work to be done, I would leave our cottage next to the dorm and go over to the student lounge and play Ping-Pong with the residents, or talk over things with them in their rooms, or just sit there and read the newspaper. I got a reputation for being a terrific resident fellow and one of the rare profs on campus who spent time with undergraduates and got to know them. What a setup—playing Ping-Pong as a way of not doing more important things and getting a reputation as Mr. Chips.

Procrastinators often follow exactly the wrong tack. They try to minimize their commitments, assuming that if they have only a few things to do, they will quit procrastinating and get them done. But this goes contrary to the basic nature of the procrastinator and destroys his most important source of motivation. The few tasks on his list will be, by definition, the most important, and the only way to avoid doing them will be to do nothing. This is a way to become a couch potato, not an effective human being.

At this point you may be asking, "How about the important tasks at the top of the list that one never does?" Admittedly, there is a potential problem here.

The trick is to pick the right sorts of projects for the top of the list. The ideal sorts of things have two characteristics. First, they seem to have clear deadlines (but really don't). Second, they seem awfully important (but really aren't). Luckily, life abounds with such tasks. In universities the vast majority of tasks fall into this category, and I'm sure the same is true for most other large institutions. Take, for example, the item at the top of my list right now. This is finishing an essay for a volume on the philosophy of language. It was supposed to have been done eleven months ago. I have accomplished an enormous number of important things as a way of not working on it. A couple of months ago, bothered by guilt, I wrote a letter to the editor saying how sorry I was to be so late and expressing my good intentions to get to work. Writing the letter was, of course, a way of not working on the article. It turned out that I really wasn't much further behind schedule than anyone else. And how important is this article anyway? Not so important that at some point something that seems more important won't come along. Then I'll get to work on it.

Another example is book order forms. I write this in June. In October I will teach a class on epistemology. The book order forms are already overdue at the bookstore.

It is easy to take this as an important task with a pressing deadline. (For you nonprocrastinators, I will point out that deadlines really start to press a week or two after they pass.) I receive almost daily reminders from the department secretary; students sometimes ask me what we will be reading; and the unfilled order form sits right in the middle of my desk, right under the empty potato chip bag. This task is near the top of my list; it bothers me and motivates me to do other useful but superficially less important things. But, in fact, the bookstore is plenty busy with forms already filed by nonprocrastinators. If I send mine in by midsummer, things will be fine. I know that I will order well-known books from efficient publishers; I always do. And no doubt I will accept some other, apparently more important, task sometime between now and, say, the first of August, at which point my psyche will feel comfortable about filling out the order forms as a way of not doing this new task.

The observant reader may feel at this point that structured procrastination requires a certain amount of self-deception, because one is in effect constantly perpetrating a pyramid scheme on oneself. Exactly. One needs to be able to recognize and commit oneself to tasks with inflated importance and unreal deadlines, while making oneself feel that these tasks are important and urgent. This is not a problem, because virtually all procrastinators have excellent self-deception skills. And what could be more noble than using one character flaw to offset the negative effects of another?

CHAPTER TWO

Procrastination and Perfectionism

Now that you have read the first chapter, if all is going according to plan, you realize that although you are a procrastinator, you are a structured procrastinator who gets a lot of valuable work done. So you have quit despising yourself. Still you may wonder if there is some way to become less of a procrastinator. In the next couple of chapters, I'll develop a few ideas that may apply to your situation and be helpful.

I received an interesting and insightful email from someone who had read about structured procrastination. This woman, whom I'll call Mistress Imelda, has her own leather fetish gear company and is writing a novel. She writes:

> I wanted to thank you for your article. My fiancé and I are both procrastinators. He sent your article to me and I could not believe how familiar I was with the things you wrote.
>
> I have experienced so much guilt and emotional torture because of my inability to follow through with my many projects or rather, my choice not to because I know I am fully capable of following through and completing my projects but for some reason, I choose not to. I associated this with my fear of failure, knowing I will not face rejection and failure as much if I do not complete the project that will be so blatantly subjected to the intense scrutiny of my own personal judgment. Being a perfectionist, getting past my own scrutiny is one of the hardest issues I face.

I have a trilogy of novels unfinished, a small leather fetish gear company with orders not filled, a demo album to start and finish, a graphic novel, numerous paintings, and sketches to do. I manage to do things like sort and clean my paintbrushes, arrange my computer for space to store my music projects that are not started, sort out my chapters and do many, many summaries on my characters and plot because all of this makes me feel as if I am getting closer to actually working on those things. I have even tried to write to prospective bands and announce that I'm working on my demo, to somehow provide myself with a goal, an actual date to be finished. When they reply, excited for me and eager to hear the demo, it only further amplifies my fear of starting and of subsequent rejection.

I am so deeply a procrastinator that I refuse to commit to any other people on projects, knowing I will let them down. This keeps me limited to only disappointing myself with my constant deviations from the important goals I have, only to work on less important ones. Your article was so very similar to the way I do things. I was shocked, even dumbfounded, that any other person could possibly do this. It brought self-understanding to me in a way no one has previously done in the area of self-motivation.

Thank you so much.

Imelda

Mistress Imelda is an insightful procrastinator because she realizes that she is a perfectionist. But which comes first—the procrastination or the perfectionism? I think perfectionism leads to procrastination. I was slow to see the connection between the two, because I don't think of myself as a perfectionist. Many procrastinators do not realize that they are perfectionists, for the simple reason that we have never done anything perfectly or even nearly so. We have never been told that something we did was perfect, nor have we ourselves felt that anything we did was perfect. We think, quite mistakenly, that being a perfectionist implies, often or sometimes, or at least once, having completed some task to perfection. But this is a misunderstanding of the basic dynamic of perfectionism.

Perfectionism of the sort I am talking about is a matter of fantasy, not reality. Here's how it works in my case. Someone wants me to do something—perhaps a publisher wants me to referee a manuscript that has been submitted, which involves giving an opinion about whether it is worth publishing and, if it is, how it might be improved. I accept the task, probably because the publisher offers to pay me with a number of free books, which I wrongly suppose that if I owned I would get around to reading.

Immediately my fantasy life kicks in. I imagine myself writing the most wonderful referee's report. I imagine giving the manuscript an incredibly thorough read and writing an evaluation that helps the author to greatly improve his efforts. I imagine the publisher getting my write-up and saying, "Wow, this is the best referee report I have ever read." I imagine my report being completely accurate, completely fair, incredibly helpful to both author and publisher.

Why do I have such fantasies? God knows. Or maybe my shrink does. Perhaps my father did not praise me enough as a child. Or maybe he heaped praise on me when once, accidentally no doubt, I accomplished some task extremely well. Perhaps such fantasies are genetic. But this is, at most, just a practical multistep program, not an attempt at psychotherapy. (The first step is to read the previous chapter, "Structured Procrastination." This is the second step. If I figure out any more steps, they will be in subsequent chapters.) So we won't worry about why I, or you, have such fantasies. The point is that if you are a procrastinator, of the garden variety sort, something like this probably goes through your mind.

This is perfectionism in the relevant sense. It's not a matter of really ever doing anything that is perfect or that even comes close. It is a matter of using tasks you accept to feed your fantasy of doing things perfectly, or at any rate, extremely well.

How does the fantasy of perfection feed procrastination? Well, it's not so easy to do things perfectly.

(At least I assume that it is not. Perhaps someday I'll do something perfectly, and then I'll know for sure.) Presumably one needs time. And the proper setting. Clearly, to referee this manuscript, I need to read it carefully. That will take quite a few hours. I want to go beyond the manuscript itself and read some of the material that the author cites, to make sure the author is accurate and fair in what he says about it. I've read book reviews by philosophers I admire, and they obviously do this. It's very impressive. I need to be over in the library to do that properly. Actually, in today's world, one doesn't need to be in the library. One can find a lot of this stuff on the Web. If one knows how. Unfortunately, I don't know how. I know that there is this thing called JSTOR that allows one to access lots of academic journals online. If you are working at Stanford you can access it through the library. But it would be nice to be able to access it at home. I may want to work late into the night on this referee job. To access JSTOR at home you need to set up something called a proxy server. I'd better figure out how to do that.

A few hours later I'm done setting up the proxy server. Most likely I am done because I have given up. Every time I think I have the thing set up, it doesn't work right, or my screen goes blank. But suppose instead that I am done because I have actually managed to make the proxy server work. One thing I will not have done is start on the referee job. I will have invested enough time to have actually given the book a quick read and to have formed an opinion of it, but I will not have done this or even gotten started. I will feel like a schmuck, and rightly so.

Then what happens? I go on to other things. Most likely, the manuscript slowly disappears under subsequent memos, mail, empty potato chip bags, piles of files, and other things that accumulate on my desk. (See the chapter on horizontal organization, page 47.) Then, in about six weeks, I get an email from the publisher, asking when she can expect the report. Maybe, if she has dealt with me before, this email arrives a bit before I promised the report. If she hasn't, it arrives a few days after the deadline.

Now, finally, I snap into action. My fantasy structure changes. I no longer picture myself writing the world's best referee report ever. I imagine some woman back in the New York office of Oxford University Press. I picture her, empty-handed, going to the editorial meeting, where she promised to have an evaluation of the manuscript. "I'm sorry," she says to her boss. "I counted on this fellow from Stanford, but he didn't come through." "That's it," her boss says. "You're fired." "But I've got three small children, my husband is in the hospital, and the mortgage is overdue," she says. "I'm sorry," he replies. "I've got a business to run." I imagine meeting this woman; she gives me a withering stare. "You cost me my job," she says.

And then there is the author. Maybe whether or not he gets tenure turns on getting this book accepted. It's probably a great book, a masterpiece that has been sitting on my desk unread while the tenure decision lies in the balance. Perhaps someday the whole world of philosophy will know that this deserving person was denied tenure because John Perry sat on his manuscript—like the editors at the physics journals who turned down Einstein's early manuscripts. (I'm not sure that ever happened—I meant to look it up but haven't gotten around to it.)

At this point, I dig through the files, magazines, and unopened correspondence on my desk, and after a bit of panic—Have I lost the manuscript? Will I have to ask the publisher for another copy? Should I lie and say that I thought I mailed the manuscript back with the review, but it must have been in that briefcase the mugger took from me?—I find it. I take a few hours, read it, write a perfectly adequate report, and then send it off.

Now let's analyze what happened. First of all, let's note that because I am a structured procrastinator, I have used the referee report as a way of doing a lot of other things. For example, perhaps I set up that proxy server. A colleague says plaintively at some point, "I'd like to access JSTOR from home, but I don't have the proxy server set up." "Oh," I exclaim jauntily, "I set mine up a couple of weeks ago. Works great." "How did you ever find the time?" he asks admiringly. I don't reply, but look smug.

Furthermore, procrastinating was a way of giving myself permission to do a less-than-perfect job on a task that didn't require a perfect job. In theory, as long as the deadline was a ways off, I had plenty of time to go to the library or set myself up for a long evening at home and do a thorough, scholarly, perfect job refereeing this book. But when the deadline was near there was no longer time to do a perfect job. I had to just sit down and do an imperfect, but adequate, job. The fantasies of perfection are replaced by the fantasies of utter failure. So I finally got to work on it.

In the end, things turned out OK. I did finish the report, it wasn't too late, the editor kept her job, the book was accepted or not, the author received tenure or not. True, the report wasn't perfect, but it was perfectly good enough. So structured procrastination seems to be working.

But still, can't we do better? Can't we avoid the emotional turmoil and the waste of everyone's time that these perfectionist fantasies lead to? It would have been simpler for me, and for the publisher and author, if I had sat down and spent four or five hours on the manuscript right off the bat. If only I had been able to give myself permission to do an imperfect job right at the outset. Is there anything we can do to bring that about?

Well, I think there is, but it does require a little self-discipline. Not a lot. What one needs to do to bring one's perfectionist fantasies under control is what I call task triage. *Triage* basically means sorting according to urgency; its most common use is in the context of decisions made by early medical responders in wars, natural disasters, and crowded emergency rooms. They need to decide which victims are hopeless, which may survive if they get immediate treatment, and which can be made comfortable and treated later. The decisions I'm talking about really aren't that similar, but I like the sound of task triage. Maybe we can think of turning down tasks as letting them die. Some can reasonably be left until later. But for many tasks, it will work out best if you get started on them, planning to do an adequate job—perhaps even a bit better than adequate—but nothing perfect.

You have to get into the habit of forcing yourself to analyze, at the time you accept a task, the costs and benefits of doing a less-than-perfect job. You must ask yourself some questions: How useful would a perfect job be here? How much more useful would it be than a merely adequate job? Or even a half-assed job? And you've got to ask yourself: What is the probability that I will really do anything like a remotely perfect job on this? And: What difference will it make to me, and to others, whether I do or not?

Often the answer will be that a less-than-perfect job will do just fine, and moreover it's all I am ever going to do anyway. So I give myself permission to do a less-than-perfect job now, rather than waiting until the task is overdue. Which means I may as well do it now. (Or at least start on it tomorrow.)

CHAPTER THREE

To-Do Lists

I f you are a structured procrastinator, you likely have vaguely in mind, or perhaps even written down somewhere, the things you ought to be accomplishing in the days, weeks, months, and perhaps even years ahead. And at the top, motivating you to do seemingly less important things will be something that seems of paramount importance but, really, for one reason or another, isn't all that crucial after all. This is what I'll call your priority list. It's a long-term list; the projects on it will occupy you for a day or a week or a month or longer, perhaps your whole life, if you have something like "Learn Chinese" at the top.

This chapter is about a different sort of list: a daily to-do list. Many procrastinators use such a list. You might think the purpose of a to-do list is to remind you what to do. And it can be useful in that way. But that is not its primary purpose. The main function of the daily to-do list is to give the procrastinator the experience of checking off tasks as they are finished. Putting a check in the box next to the item, or crossing it out with a flourish, gives one a little psychological lift. It helps us to think of ourselves as doers, accomplishers, and not just lazy slugs. It gives us psychological momentum.

You can use your computer to make your to-do list. In fact various programs and websites—for example, Outlook, Gmail, and LazyMeter.com—will generate nice lists for you. But they are not optimal because usually the task simply disappears when you check it off. It would be much more satisfying if a big red line were drawn through the task, accompanied by a little noise of triumph, but I haven't found a program that does this.

I try to make a to-do list before I go to bed and then leave it by the clock. It starts like this:

1. TURN OFF THE ALARM.

2. DON'T HIT THE SNOOZE BUTTON.

3. GET OUT OF BED.

4. GO TO THE BATHROOM.

5. DON'T GET BACK IN BED.

6. GO DOWNSTAIRS.

7. MAKE COFFEE.

By the time I sit down with my first cup of coffee, I can check off seven items. This feels good and looks impressive. My day of accomplishment is off to a flying start. I don't need reminders to do any of these things. But I do need a little pat on the back for doing them. The only likely way of getting that pat is by having a to-do list, so I can cross off completed tasks.

The system of breaking tasks down into small increments, and giving yourself a good pat on the back for achieving each of them, has solid credentials. The *Tao Te Ching* tells us to "accomplish the great task by a series of small acts." I found this quote in Robert Maurer's book *One Small Step Can Change Your Life: The Kaizen Way*. Kaizen is a Japanese philosophy of continuous improvement through small, implementable steps. If you say you are adopting the Kaizen Way, rather than simply that you are trying to procrastinate less, you will sound like you have adopted a martial arts regimen. That's kind of cool.

Breaking big daunting tasks into smaller, less daunting ones is crucial on those occasions—rare but awful—when the structured procrastination system breaks down. For one reason or another that big task, the not doing of which has been motivating you to do other things, now absolutely must be taken care of. Here is a story the novelist Anne Lamott tells in her book for writers, *Bird by Bird*:

Thirty years ago my older brother, who was ten years old at the time, was trying to get a report on birds written that he'd had three months to write, which was due the next day. . . . He was at the kitchen table close to tears, surrounded by binder paper and pencils and unopened books on birds, immobilized by the hugeness of the task ahead. Then my father sat down beside him, put his arm around my brother's shoulder, and said, "Bird by bird, buddy. Just take it bird by bird."

Whether the tasks are large or small, unusual or just recurring items of everyday drudgery, break them down into smaller, less demanding, subtasks. Take them bird by bird. Or wing by wing, if necessary. This will make your daily to-do list pretty detailed. Easy tasks at the beginning will help you get the feelings of accomplishment flowing. The list should include do-nots along with the dos. For example:

8. POUR A SECOND CUP OF COFFEE.

9. SIT DOWN AT THE DESK, NOT ON THE
   COUCH.

10. TURN ON THE COMPUTER.

11. DO NOT CHECK EMAIL.

12. DO NOT START SURFING THE WEB.

13. OPEN WORD.

14. GO TO DOCUMENTS AND SELECT DUMMETT
    REVIEW.

This is my list for today. I made it through "Open Word" successfully. Then I came to "Dummett Review." Michael Dummett was a very important philosopher who wrote a little book on a big topic with the title *Thought and Reality*. I have agreed to review it for *Mind*, a fine British philosophy journal. I've read the book through several times, and I've even started the review. But it's hard finishing it. Reviewing an important book by an important philosopher for a top journal is pretty daunting. It's high on my priority list. It's way overdue—but in the philosophy business, the top journals seem to be used to missed deadlines. Philosophers are a pretty flaky crowd, I'm afraid. I'm definitely not the only structured procrastinator the journal has to deal with. At any rate, I couldn't finish it again today. So instead I am working on this chapter—structured procrastination at work.

Practice defensive to-do list making—spend a little time thinking about how your day could get derailed in the early stages and put in safeguards to circumvent that. Last night I saw *When Harry Met Sally* on TV. I knew there would be a good chance I'd want to start off this morning by googling "Meg Ryan," to see if there are some other movies of hers that I'd forgotten about and would like to see. Once I start googling, I seldom stop simply because I find what I was originally looking for:

I see Meg was married to Dennis Quaid. Now which Quaid brother is that? I'll check "Dennis Quaid" on Wikipedia. Ah, the handsome one. I should have guessed. Look at that, his father

was a cousin of Gene Autry! Haven't thought
about Gene Autry in a long time. Remember
"Tumbling Tumbleweeds"? Great song. I wonder
if I can get it on iTunes. . . .

And on and on. It's best to short-circuit this whole
waste of time by putting "Don't google 'Meg Ryan'"
on the to-do list, along with other reminders not to
get derailed. (I'll delve more deeply into the dangers
of Web surfing in Chapter 5.)

Follow this advice, and to-do lists can be helpful.
They won't cure procrastination, but they are part of
the strategy of self-manipulation that can help make the
procrastinator into a productive human being.

I want to emphasize again that one must make
the to-do list in advance, preferably the night before
(although not so early that you lose it before you have
a chance to put it by the alarm clock). Before you go
to sleep, you can probably imagine yourself waking
up and getting a lot done. Don't wait until the alarm
goes off to start thinking about what you want to be

committed to doing for the day. If you do, your list might consist of "turn over and go back to sleep."

And one final note about alarm clocks. We structured procrastinators may be inclined to turn them off and roll over and go back to sleep. Many come with snooze buttons, which makes this even easier to do. But if you could reach from your bed to hit the snooze button once, you can do it a second time, and a third time. It's best to have a second alarm clock, a very loud one, set for two minutes later than the first, which you put in the kitchen near the coffeepot.

CHAPTER FOUR

Get Rhythm

" Get Rhythm" is a great song by Johnny Cash. A shoeshine boy advises the Man in Black to "get rhythm when you get the blues." Not only is that good advice, but it is the fourth step in this program. I don't mean that you should work to attain a sense of rhythm if you lack one, though that is an admirable goal. I myself have evidence that I am a little deficient in this dimension. Often when there is rhythmic clapping going on in the late innings at a San Francisco

Giants game to encourage the players to extend some rally, I look around and notice that I am half a beat off. My hands are clapping when everyone else's are flying away from each other, and vice versa. This is embarrassing, but it doesn't mean that I am not getting the same lift in spirits as everyone else.

It's pretty obvious that music has a direct connection with emotions. We describe music with emotional terms like *sad* and *happy*. We sing lullabies to our children to calm them down—or, in the case of people like me with tin ears and little sense of rhythm, we play recordings of lullabies. Singing or humming along calms us down, too. Marching music makes us feel like marching, or at least feel better about marching if for some reason we have to march. And a happy song with an infectious beat can get us up and at 'em when we're feeling down in the dumps, which can be all too often for procrastinators.

Indeed many of us procrastinators suffer real bouts of depression. Whether the procrastination causes the depression or vice versa, I don't know. Whichever comes first, they reinforce each other. Some cases of depression require psychotherapy, or drugs, or both. Nevertheless, judging by my own case, often the right music can help a lot. And it costs a lot less.

But therein lies a problem. The wrong music can make things worse. When you're blue and moving slow, you need to hear "Start Me Up" by the Rolling Stones or Aretha Franklin's "Respect" or—if you're sticking with Johnny Cash—"Tennessee Flat Top Box." It won't help to hear him sing "Hurt," his song about injuring himself to see if he can still feel pain.

But something like "Hurt" is just what you are in the mood for when the blues hit. That's why they call the blues the blues, I suppose. I get up feeling low. Two or three or four cups of coffee don't get me going. Maybe music will help? Oh look, I've got a John Lee Hooker album so I can hear him sing about how whiskey and women—or wimmin, to be exact—wrecked his life. That won't help much.

What I need to hear is something like "Seventy-six Trombones" from *The Music Man*. I hear that song and things start to brighten. The rhythm makes me want to get up and move. Images of Professor Harold Hill leading the River City Boys' Band through an idealized Iowa town stir memories of high school bands at halftime—memories somehow oddly disconnected from the miseries actually involved in attending high school. So the answer seems simple: If you wake up feeling blue, put "Seventy-six Trombones" on the old turntable or into your CD player, or select it from your iTunes library or whatever it is that you do to listen to music.

But who makes music choices like that when you wake up depressed in the morning? Here is where technology can help. It doesn't have to be something Steve Jobs came up with. The old-fashioned clock radio will do, as long as you can find a station that plays reasonably perky music in the early morning. You tune to that station the night before. It doesn't matter if you like the music it plays. You may hate it. Maybe you are an anarchist and the last thing you want to hear in the morning is "Stars and Stripes Forever." Maybe you are an Anglophobe and don't want to hear the Rolling Stones singing "Start Me Up." None of this matters. Choose a perky station; turn the volume up loud, put the clock radio a fair distance from your bed, and it will get you going. You wouldn't make these choices in the morning. But you can make these choices for yourself the night before.

There are, of course, plenty of upbeat songs that any reasonable person shouldn't mind having inflicted on them, even if they really aren't in the mood to hear them. A lot of classics fit the bill nicely. By classics I mean rock and some country music from the 1960s, '70s, and '80s. On the radio these are now called oldies. I have no idea why. Benny Goodman, Bing Crosby, and Nat King Cole are oldies. My parents listened to them. The Stones, the Beatles, the Eagles—that's just good classic music. Anyone should acknowledge that.

Nowadays you don't have to depend on the choices of some chirpy early morning disc jockey at your local radio station. You can put together a list of exactly the songs you think will help get you off to a good start.

Of course, you need to figure out the list during some rare moment when you are in a relatively good and upbeat mood.

You can use music to help combat procrastination in other ways as well. Combine it with the bird-by-bird strategy of the last chapter. Say you need to clean out the garage. It's a huge task; you aren't going to do it all at once. But with the right music, you can get started. Resolve to begin and keep working on it for the length of your favorite CD. Even better, make a garage-cleaning playlist of energizing, cheerful tunes—the kind of songs that might even make you *want* to sort through old tools. Of course, there are dangers here. You might decide to go through your library of music to look for the perfect songs before you get started. Then you may end up organizing your music rather than your garage.

Putting a song on your start-me-up list is not a judgment about which songs and groups are the best. Perhaps you think "Hey Jude" by the Beatles is clearly superior to their song "Ob-La-Di, Ob-La-Da." The latter still might be a better choice for morning music. I happen to think Neil Diamond is right up there with Beethoven, but even if you don't, you have to admit that a lot of his songs are very energizing. The group Katrina and the Waves isn't in the Rock and Roll Hall of Fame, but "Walking on Sunshine" is hard to beat as a pump-you-up song. The absolute best wake-up song, in my humble opinion, is Lacy J. Dalton's "Black Coffee."

This song illustrates that, contrary to what some earlier examples may have suggested, songs with a blue, depressing, or even psychotically dysfunctional message may work fine on the list, as long as the rhythm is good. "Black Coffee"'s message isn't exactly upbeat. The toast is burning, the rain is pouring, and Dalton feels like she's losing her lover—but she does have coffee to go with all of this misery. In spite of the morose message, the rhythm is completely infectious; you will just think about drinking black coffee and getting energized and not be caught up in Dalton's various woes.

CHAPTER FIVE

The Computer and the Procrastinator

In one way, the computer is a great thing for the procrastinator. Procrastinators tend to finish tasks at the last minute at best, shortly before the absolute-and-final no-more-extensions deadline for delivery. If the final product is the kind of thing that can be emailed, the last minute can be even closer to the absolute deadline than in the bad old days, when it had to go by U.S. mail, or even the not-quite-so-bad, not-quite-so-old days when overnight by FedEx was the fastest way. Now you email it, and it gets there instantly. If you have the good fortune of living in Asia or Europe or even on the East Coast and you are meeting a deadline set by someone on the West Coast, it can even arrive before you send it.

But the computer is also a bane for the procrastinator, because it makes sinking time in utterly worthless pursuits tempting and easy. The big problems are coping with email and surfing the Web.

When it comes to email, I must admit I haven't come up with any good techniques for dealing with the special dangers it provides for the procrastinator. I hope that talking about my difficulties will at least make others with similar problems feel they are not alone. On the temptation to spend endless hours on the Web, however, I do have some suggestions based on my vast experience of giving in to it.

The Agony and Ecstasy of Email

Back in the days when most correspondence came in envelopes delivered by the letter carrier, I wasn't much good at keeping up. There was a certain regular rhythm to things. Mail came in, and I started opening it. For some reason or another, I sat down and dealt with certain items promptly. Other things, like bills, were put in a pile that I absolutely had to attend to once a month, and I eventually developed the habit of paying them on time, since the consequences of not doing so were so dire. Other stuff—some opened, some unopened—piled up toward the back of the desk to be dealt with "later." Eventually letters would begin to fall off the back of the desk to the floor, where they went unnoticed for long periods of time, perhaps forever. In this way the pile stayed manageable, a repository for finding tasks to do as a way of not doing other more urgent things that came along.

Occasionally this system led to unfortunate results. Some letters that fell off the back of the desk or remained in the pile but were never opened turned out to be important. But not too many of them. If answering a letter was truly essential to someone, I would usually get a phone call or a follow-up letter from that person, and then I would search for the original and deal with it. And even I am not stupid enough to overlook letters from, say, the Internal Revenue Service that are marked urgent.

This system was far from perfect, but sometimes it had its upsides. For a while, when I was a young assistant professor at UCLA, I was in charge of admissions to the M.A. program. It wasn't a very big program, and I tended to let things pile up until the chair of the department reminded me that it was time to bring a list of the best candidates to the next meeting. About ten years later, after I had left UCLA, I was trying to raise some money for a research institute at Stanford. I had lunch with the CEO of a Silicon Valley company that made high-quality modems. This was in the day when all people who wanted to use a computer from home dialed in to a mainframe, and a 1200-baud modem was state of the art, an expensive bit of equipment that everyone wanted. His company made the best ones. He was very successful.

During lunch, it emerged that he had been a philosophy major at a state college in California and had applied to UCLA to get a master's degree. He did so only because he couldn't figure out what else to do upon graduation. He never heard from UCLA, but while he was waiting he started his modem company, from which he made a fortune. I said I thought I knew what had happened. His letter had come to me, been piled at the back of the desk, and fallen off—and thus was never dealt with. I felt bad, momentarily.

But this fellow was very grateful for the way I handled his case. Earning a master of arts in philosophy, even from UCLA, doesn't usually lead to fame and fortune, especially for those who choose to do so only because they can't figure out what else to do with their lives. So things had worked out very well for him. He didn't give any money to the research institute, but he did give me a top-of-the-line 1200-baud modem.

Now you might think email would change the way I handle mail for the better. It is a lot easier to answer email than old-fashioned mail. Nevertheless, at least in my case, the psychology of the structured procrastinator has easily outwitted modern technology.

Most of my mail now shows up not on my desk but in my in-box on my computer. I use Gmail, which does a good job cleaning out spam and diverting stuff into files that I don't want automatically deleted, but I'm sure I will only get around to when I'm in a real procrastinatory funk—things like reports from my congresswoman, or descriptions of the latest assault on the environment from forests.com, or minutes from Rotary meetings.

The rest piles up in my in-box. For whatever reason, I deal with most—but never quite all—of my email the day it comes in. I try to get to some of the unanswered items every so often, especially when the number of emails in my in-box gets close to 100. People send me little messages suggesting that their previous email must have gotten lost, so I search for that earlier note and try to respond to it. But just like the letters that used to fall off the back of my desk, there is a certain amount of stuff that remains undealt with for long periods of time. Sometimes, when I finally get to these emails, I feel very bad for having ignored them. Luckily, I cope fairly well with guilt. And for every email I ignore for months, there is one that I deal with immediately, as a way of not doing something more important, sending back a reply so quickly that the recipient is amazed at my promptness.

I've tried to use the resources of email to manage things better. I started a file called Really Urgent Stuff That Must Not Be Ignored and forced myself for a while to put everything that seemed important, but that I didn't want to deal with the very day it came in, into this file. But then I forgot about it, only to stumble on it months later.

Gmail lets you click a little star on a message and then archive it. It disappears from your in-box, which gives you a sense of accomplishment. But it's not like throwing it in the trash. Later, when you are in a mood to get a lot done, you can select the file of starred messages, and that list appears instead of your in-box. This seemed like a great way to flag the important stuff that I wasn't ready to deal with but wanted to get out of my in-box. But it just led to a second list about as long as the in-box, so there wasn't any gain. The occasions when I felt ambitious and loaded up my starred messages turned out to be rather rare.

The structured procrastinator has an advantage in avoiding one of the worst dangers of email. In the old days, if you got a letter, even if you sat down and answered it right away, there would be a four- to six-day interval before you could expect a response. But there seems to be a certain group of people out there who send a follow-up the minute they receive a response, putting the ball back in your court. This can be very frustrating to a procrastinator, who hasn't finished patting himself on the back for answering one email when another one arrives from the same person. Such people learn that I am not one of them, for even if I answered the original email promptly, I will almost certainly procrastinate on the follow-up. This is frustrating for the gung-ho correspondent, and some of them eliminate procrastinators from their lists of regular correspondents. Unfortunately, not all of them learn the lesson.

Surfing Without Drowning

Some correspondents helpfully embed links to pertinent websites in their emails, and following these links can be something of a rabbit hole. You can end up spending hours investigating websites, jumping from one to another, and then suddenly discover that the sun has set and the day is over. Sometimes this pays unexpected dividends. You develop little pools of expertise, perhaps about the sort of metal roofing that is available for a barn—if one has a barn, which I don't—or the history of Tajikistan. These pools of expertise occasionally prove useful in conversation or when working a crossword puzzle. But it is easy to lose an hour or two procrastinating without having anything to show for it—or a day or two, for that matter.

Surfing from irrelevant link to even more irrelevant link is a bit like watching junk TV. It's very hard to stop watching a junky program by simply relying on willpower. I've waited for the better part of an hour just to see how much they charge for a Ginsu knife, or green bags that keep your vegetables fresh, or a bottle opener that looks like a bass and plays "99 Bottles of Beer" when you use it, even though I have no intention of ordering any of those things. What is needed is something to break the spell, like lunch, or an urgent need to go to the bathroom, or a completely boring commercial, or any program involving Paris Hilton or Glenn Beck doing anything whatsoever.

I've learned one trick that helps when I am going to be on the Web, and thus inevitably tempted to surf. I try to start my session only when some natural event is sure to interrupt me. I log on when I'm already hungry or I'm pretty sure my wife is going to pop in with some urgent task before too long or I am already feeling the first signs of a full bladder. If you use a laptop, another ploy is to unplug it before you start your email; the spell will be broken when the battery dies—although as batteries improve, this technique becomes less useful.

If nothing else works, set an alarm clock to interrupt you after an hour. Of course, you may end up knowing a little less about Tajikistan than you would have liked.

CHAPTER SIX

A Plea for the Horizontally Organized

There is nothing intrinsically disabling about being left-handed, but when the world is organized for right-handers, it can be a real handicap. Consider the chairs one finds in university lecture halls, with little fold-up desktops on the right side for taking notes. A left-hander has to write with her left elbow dangling in midair or turn all squeezed around in her seat, with her elbow where the right-hander puts the notebook and her notebook on the narrow back of the desk where the right-hander puts his elbow. We might call being left-handed a situational handicap; in situations where things are set up with right-handed people in mind, being left-handed is a disadvantage.

I am not left-handed, but I have another less well-known situational handicap. I am a horizontal organizer in a world set up for vertical organizers. This is worth discussing here because in my experience, a high proportion of structured procrastinators are also horizontal organizers.

The idea of vertical organization comes from tall, vertical filing cabinets. Someday these will only be a dim memory, as the whole world will be paperless. But filing cabinets still occupy many offices. As far as the horizontal organizer is concerned, they are strange reminders of a different way of life. But vertical organizers actually use them. Indeed, the main mark of a vertical organizer is the ability to make use of these things. Here is some cheery advice from Sally Allen, who writes a blog on getting organized:

Keep the paper flowing to its final destination. Oops, you say there is no final destination? Well, my friends, that is what piles are made of—lost paper looking for a home. . . . Creating a filing system that works for you is like finding the pot of gold at the end of the rainbow. A good filing system will put you back in control, enhance your professional image, and increase productivity.

I'm sure Sally Allen is a lovely person and that she is right about this. But she is a vertical organizer. Vertical organizers find it natural to use filing cabinets to store materials that they intend to use just an hour or a day or a week later. When they need that stuff again, they reach into the filing cabinet, pull out the folder and resume working on it. They don't understand how foreign this whole idea is to a horizontal organizer.

The other day I was working on a letter to the Palo Alto Medical Clinic explaining why my bill is screwed up and I don't owe them as much money as they think I do. It's pretty complicated stuff, and I had bills and correspondence spread out in front of me. I wasn't able to finish by the time I had to leave. A vertical organizer would have scooped this stuff up, and put it in a file to retrieve later. Had I done this, there might have been a bare spot on my desk. These bare spots are the mark of vertical organizers. They are a dead giveaway.

Now of course that is not what I did at all. I left the unfinished letter on my desk, with the materials spread out. Actually, they were not exactly *on* the desk, because some other ongoing projects were already spread there; the letter and supporting documents were on top of half-graded papers, half-written lectures, half-read brochures, and the like.

The fact is, I am a horizontal organizer. I like all the things I am working on spread out on a surface in front of me, where they can beckon me to continue working on them. When I put something in a file, I never see it again. The problem isn't that I can't find it (although that has happened) but that I don't look. I am constitutionally incapable of opening a filing cabinet and fishing out a half-finished project to resume working on it.

You might think that computers would take care of this, but they don't, as we saw in the last chapter. The horizontal organizer leaves everything on her computer desktop, which can end up as messy as a real one. As I explained earlier, when someone like me turns to email, she is only capable of dealing with what is in her in-box. If she makes a file and labels it "Urgent Stuff," it won't work. She'll never get around to opening the file.

I do use filing cabinets. They are a place to (1) store finished projects that one plans never to look at again and (2) put things that one would feel bad about tossing but has no intention of reading. Say a former colleague sends you a long boring paper that she has just finished. It would be unfeeling and mean to throw it away; plus, you would no doubt have to lie the next time you saw her. But if you put the essay in a filing cabinet, you can say, "Yes, it's in my file of things to read this summer." This implies no more than that you have a file labeled "things to read this summer" and that you put the paper in it. So you are not really telling a lie, even if the chances of reading the paper this summer (or any summer, fall, winter, or spring) are nil.

Now looking as it does, my desk is likely to attract critical comments from vertical organizers such as Sally Allen. These people tend to think that a desk spread thick with paper is the sign of a disorganized person. But this isn't so. It's like looking at a left-handed student all squashed up taking notes on one of those aforementioned desks and thinking that he is uncoordinated. The problem is that he is at a situational disadvantage. And that is the problem for horizontal organizers, too. The whole world is set up to help keep vertically organized people on top of things, through the use of filing cabinets. The only things horizontally organized people have are desks, the tops of filing cabinets, nearby chairs, and the floor. If some thought were put into a good document storage and retrieval system for horizontally organized people, we could be as organized and neat as anyone else.

Here is my idea. Instead of a desk, I would like to have a very large lazy Susan in my office like the ones they have at the large round tables at Chinese restaurants. The lazy Susan is a rotating circular platform above the table, covering most of it, leaving just enough room for the plates of the diners around the edge. The various dishes are put on the lazy Susan, which can be spun (at a low speed, unless one wants moo goo gai pan all over one's shirt) so that each diner has access to each dish.

I think something about fifteen feet in diameter would be about right for my office. My whole life would be spread out on this lazy Susan. It could have little pie-shaped areas labeled with letters of the alphabet. When I had gotten as far as I could with the letter to the medical clinic, I would have just turned the lazy Susan around to the right pizza-slice-shaped section and placed the materials there. (I suppose the right letter would be *M* for "medical." Maybe *C* for "clinic." Or maybe *L* for "letter" or *U* for "unfinished" or *S* for "something I'm upset about." I'm sure that if I had a lazy Susan I would get the knack of making this sort of decision.)

With my projects laid out on my lazy Susan, they would each have a claim on my attention that they'd never have if they were filed away. And yet they would be neatly organized, just as organized as if I were a vertical organizer.

Admittedly, a fifteen-foot lazy Susan would take up a lot of space in my office, which measures sixteen by sixteen feet. I kind of imagine myself like people I have seen in photos of model railroad clubs. The whole room is taken up with the board for the train—little towns, papier-mâché mountains, and lots of track running everywhere. The operator ducks under all of this and pops up in the middle somewhere. Because lazy Susans are round and my office is square, my chair would presumably be in one of the spaces left in the corners. I could come in, crawl under the lazy Susan to the corner, and pop up ready to work as efficiently and neatly as a vertically organized person. I could also wear one of those denim engineer caps like model railroaders do, although I suppose that is not strictly necessary to make the system work.

CHAPTER SEVEN

Collaborating with the Enemy?

Perhaps the best way to overcome procrastination is to team up with people who aren't procrastinators. And no, nonprocrastinators are not the enemy. On the contrary. We get on their nerves, justifiably so in many cases. And their normal working habits can seem foreign and threatening to us. But when it comes to getting stuff done, such people can work even better than alarm clocks, although, of course, they can be harder to turn off. I've written several things with people who aren't procrastinators, and it has worked pretty well. In the 1980s I wrote a book with my late friend, the brilliant logician Jon Barwise. Barwise's approach to writing was to figure out what he wanted to say, prepare an outline, start writing, and continue working until he was done. I don't know how he came up with such a bizarre system. He expected the parts I agreed to write to be done more or less on the same schedule as the parts he agreed to write. This was hard on our friendship but worked well for finishing the book. Barwise's method and how well it worked for him was a revelation to me, and I resolved to be more like him—but it didn't work out.

Years ago I had an idea for a public radio talk show about philosophy that I would call *Philosophy Talk*. The idea itself gave me great pleasure, but of course I did nothing to bring it about. Then I mentioned it to my friend Ken Taylor. Like me, Ken is a member of the Philosophy Department at Stanford. And also like me, he has a good face for radio. We both love the philosophy of language. But in many important ways he is totally unlike me and most other philosophers. He is a real type-A, nonprocrastinating go-getter. Before I knew what was happening, he had us asking Stanford for money for a pilot and attending public radio conventions. We got some funds, made a pilot, and went to a convention where we cornered program directors and explained our great idea. They pretty much looked at us unbelievingly and explained how even the public radio audience wouldn't want to spend an hour of their time listening to philosophers talk about free will, or the existence of God, or nihilism, or whether numbers were real. I was discouraged and ready to give up. But Ken pushed on until we found Ben Manilla, a radio producer with lots of energy and contacts and, like Ken, no gift for procrastination.

Now we have a radio program called *Philosophy Talk*, which is carried by a lot of stations and has a large and appreciative audience. (Go to philosophytalk.org if, contrary to the wisdom of most program directors, this sounds interesting to you.) Every week there is a conference call to plan future shows. Ken has enlisted students to provide us with ideas for themes, possible guests, and information on the topics. Every Sunday morning we drive to San Francisco to broadcast the show at 10 a.m. from the lovely studios of KALW. A situation has been created in which even I cannot very well procrastinate.

Like setting an alarm clock, teaming up with non-procrastinating collaborators is a way of putting the decision to get to work out of one's immediate control. The downside, of course, is that one ends up working pretty hard.

You may ask, what happens when procrastinators collaborate? Two structured procrastinators can accomplish quite a bit, as long as the tasks they are putting off and the ones they are working on line up pretty well. My current collaborator is Kepa Korta, a Basque philosopher. He is definitely a procrastinator, although not to the same degree as I am. Nevertheless we have finally finished a book, *Critical Pragmatics*, only about a year later than we had planned. I can't quite figure out how we managed to get it done, but we did.

Another one of my collaborators, David Israel, is not a procrastinator. Perhaps he once was. If so, he overcame the habit long ago. He is a computer scientist with a regular day job in the industry. He does, however, have a different flaw, which I may have been the first to diagnose. He has what I call right-parenthesis deficit disorder. David's head is usually so full of ideas—and in particular, objections to whatever I have just said—that he can't finish one thought before starting another. A typical reply to an insight of mine goes like this:

You are right about the need for that distinction (although, by the way, quite confused about why we need the distinction (which actually isn't quite the right distinction (of course there are big problems about what exactly a distinction is anyway. . . .

There is no shortage of left parentheses, but on his own, David never manages to come up with the right parentheses necessary to close his myriad thoughts.

We work well together, however, because my mind wanders off after the first couple of digressions and works on completing whatever was the most plausible thought he started, ignoring the rest. The conversation continues like this, and eventually we get somewhere and even have finished a few things. Working with David is so much fun that it is almost painless, in spite of his inability to finish a sentence and his insistence on actually getting things done.

Most of the collaborators I have had the luck to work with tended to be just ever so slightly compulsive. When a task comes up, they set to work on it. One of my guiding principles has always been never to redo work that some competent person is already doing. As hard as I try to overcome my procrastinating habits, there is likely to be a short pause between the time when it becomes clear that some task needs to be done for a joint project and the moment when I plunge into doing it. Often enough, my collaborator has already started. I don't complain.

So, if you have chosen your collaborators well, they—unable to resist—will likely have already started on many tasks by the time you are ready to plunge in. This doesn't necessarily mean that you will do less than your share. Make it your job to compliment your collaborators on the good work they are doing. Be sure they know you are aware of all that they accomplish while you are procrastinating. Use your skills as a structured procrastinator to do lots of relatively unimportant tasks that the nonprocrastinator might never get around to. Buy lunch. Play some music. Keep them happy.

CHAPTER EIGHT

Fringe Benefits

One of the great fringe benefits of being a structured procrastinator is that sometimes an important task toward the top of one's list simply disappears. One morning not long ago I was supposed to work on a reference letter for a former student. It had been a dozen or so years since he'd earned his PhD; he was now a full professor at a college in a nice but dull town—an ideal place to raise kids, as we say. Now that his kids were grown up, he wanted to find a job in a less ideal place to raise kids. So I agreed to write a letter. Not exactly a daunting task but still a significant one.

But then that morning he sent great news. All the jobs he'd applied for were the kind that would ask for references directly, after narrowing down their list of candidates. I didn't have to write a letter after all. I could put it off until someone asked. That might take months. Found time! Well, not exactly, because I might have been doing the same thing I was doing even if I hadn't gotten the email. At any rate I didn't spend my day not writing something I was supposed to be writing. So I was given the gift of guilt-free time.

In Chapter 1 we looked at how good self-deception skills could benefit a structured procrastinator, motivating her to do useful things as a way of not doing very important things, which ultimately really aren't all that important. But sometimes, like that day, good self-deception skills aren't necessary. The world just gives you a little bonus for procrastinating. I could have written that letter when it was first asked for, a few weeks earlier. Instead, I put it off, assuming that as the need for it came near, I would get a reminder (or two or three). Had I written it early on, it might have been a complete waste of time. Or it might have been a partial waste of time—my former student might write another article or get another grant before a letter is solicited, and then I'd have to rewrite it. There is a small chance that I'd lose the letter, misfiling it or accidentally deleting it or suffering a hard disk failure before it was backed up. It's also possible that the world, or the academic profession, might come to an end before it was needed.

In the 2011 movie *Melancholia*, a planet by that name crashes into the Earth and destroys it. It's clear for a while in advance of the cataclysm that this is going to happen. Kirsten Dunst plays a very depressed young woman living with her reasonably well-adjusted sister and brother-in-law and their young son. We see how much better the depressed Kirsten Dunst copes with the impending end of the world than her well-adjusted family members; her melancholy allows her to deal with the fears of her nephew. My theory is that her depression included a good dose of procrastination, and her calmness and serenity were due to thinking about all the stupid tasks she didn't waste time on. I wouldn't want to say the end of the world was a fringe benefit of her procrastination, but the calmness and serenity were.

There is an old adage, "Never put off until tomorrow what you can do today." This is quite absurd. Let's assume that each day ends at midnight. As long as it isn't yet midnight, according to this adage, you should be working on something, even if you could just as well do it tomorrow. Among other things, this means you won't see *The Daily Show with Jon Stewart* or *Late Show with David Letterman*—unless you count those as tasks. So you will be totally out of touch with current events and important cultural trends. It also means you will never get to sleep before midnight, unless there is absolutely nothing you could be doing today rather than tomorrow. It really is silly advice.

Better advice is, "Never do today any task that may disappear by tomorrow." But if you are a structured procrastinator, you don't need that advice. You will comply with it automatically. It's like a fringe benefit.

What the tasks on your priority list are supposed to do is disappear. One way for this to happen is for you to do them. But there are other ways for them to disappear. Someone else might do them. If you just sit on a task you are supposed to do, waiting for someone else to get impatient and do it, that's manipulative and annoying. But perhaps if you don't exactly rush to do it, it will give someone who really wants to do it a chance. For example, the chair of the department asks me to come up with some suggestions for a speaker for next year's Kant Lecture—a prestigious invited lecture sponsored by the department. She wants an annotated list, giving lots of information about each candidate, that the department can then discuss. This is the sort of assignment I hate. It involves evaluating people, choosing between them, and defending one's choices at the department meeting.

But it is just the sort of thing that other people love to do. So I give the task a couple days to disappear, or at least get simpler, on its own. Sure enough, other department members begin to feed me suggestions, accompanied by lengthy write-ups. They have done the thinking and evaluating. I paste together their emails and edit down the evaluations, giving my colleagues plenty of credit, and the report is pretty much done. I won't have to defend anything, because my colleagues will defend their own choices. Maybe I add an obscure name or two to prove that I was actively involved in the process. I pick a couple of people to whom I would like to be in a position to say, "I put your name forward for the Kant Lecture." They won't rise to the level of being actively discussed, so I won't have to defend my suggestions.

Some tasks disappear because events make them irrelevant. After the San Francisco Giants won the World Series in 2010, I vowed I would get play-off tickets for 2011. Of course, I didn't quite get around to it before they were eliminated from the pennant race and even the wild card slot. Thank goodness I didn't plunge into that task prematurely!

Sometimes if you wait a bit before jumping into a project, you may find out something useful about how it should be done. I need to get a new printer for my computer. That means a trip to Fry's or someplace similar, where I will be overwhelmed with choices. Laser or inkjet? Black-and-white or color? Pay almost nothing for a printer that will then require expensive cartridges or pay a lot up front for one that is cheaper to operate? Do I care if it can print envelopes or four-by-six photos? And should it also fax and scan? When is the last time I sent a fax? Or scanned something? Will the printer work with the new Mac operating system? For that matter, will I ever get around to installing the new Mac operating system? Probably best to read up on printers on the Internet or in *Consumer Reports*. But I'd rather chew on thumbtacks than read up on printers in *Consumer Reports*.

Fortunately the world is full of people who know more than I do about these things, or at least have firm opinions. I'm having lunch tomorrow with a colleague who is sure to have lots of advice about printers. The advice may be worthless, but if I follow his advice, at least I won't have to blame myself if things don't work out. Or I can ask my neighbor, an obsessive reader of *Consumer Reports*. He's an engineer, and therefore, in my mind, authoritative about all things technical. I'm sure to see him before long. No need to go to Fry's today. No need to read up on printers. No need to even think about printers. Let the situation mature. This kind of useful thinking comes naturally to the structured procrastinator.

Now maybe I need to be a little careful here. I've been trying to make procrastinators feel less guilty about their delaying ways, because they are most likely structured procrastinators who are actually getting quite a lot done. In this chapter I've been considering actual benefits of being a procrastinator. But I don't want to take this too far.

When I was a young philosopher, I asked a senior colleague, Pat Suppes (then and now a famous philosopher of science and an astute student of human nature), what the secret of happiness was. Instead of giving me advice, he made a rather droll observation about what a lot of people who were happy with themselves seem to have done, namely:

1. Take a careful inventory of their shortcomings and flaws
2. Adopt a code of values that treats these things as virtues
3. Admire themselves for living up to it

Brutal people admire themselves for being manly; compulsive pedants admire themselves for their attention to detail; naturally selfish and mean people admire themselves for their dedication to helping the market reward talent and punish failure, and so on.

I don't want my fellow procrastinators to fall into this trap. Procrastination is a flaw, not a well-hidden virtue. The goal isn't to find a philosophy of life that makes procrastinators into heroes (although it might be fun to try to work out the principles). I simply want to note that it's not the worst flaw in the world; you can be a procrastinator and still get a lot of work done. Plus, with good self-deception skills and the little bit of willpower that allows you to manipulate yourself, you can become less of a procrastinator. And finally—the point of this chapter—sometimes the flaw has its benefits.

CHAPTER NINE

Do Procrastinators Have to Be Annoying?

For a number of years, Chapter 1 was posted on my webpage. A woman read the essay and sent her husband (I'll call him Neil) a link to it, and he in turn sent me the following email:

> My wife, a procrastinator, sent me a link to your essay
> on structured procrastination. She finds it amusing.
> I find it annoying. Perhaps it provides an effective
> way to deal with procrastination. But it does not

explain the phenomenon, nor does it speculate on why it is far more common in the groves of academe than elsewhere. As a college teacher myself, I have noticed that many of my colleagues sit on essays for weeks, foul up the grade reporting process with late submissions, and drive the bookstore batty with delays of weeks and even months. Why? I suspect part of the reason is the spirit of perversity that Dostoyevsky described in *Notes from Underground*—an impulse to engage in self-harmful behavior simply to prove that one is not a machine. But I think the main cause is academic arrogance, the belief that ordinary rules do not apply to the great thinkers, even if flouting those rules results in harm to others. So I think your essay is neither humorous nor helpful but rather is a symptom of one of the major problems in higher education.

Neil reminds us of an important point, as if we needed it, that we procrastinators get on the nerves of other people—in particular, our spouses and colleagues. It sounds as if Neil is not himself a procrastinator. But experience shows that procrastinators can even annoy other procrastinators, especially the ones to whom they are married. One just has to be a bit worse of a procrastinator than one's spouse. Even that may not be necessary.

Neil's diagnosis is that one of the reasons we procrastinators indulge in self-harmful behavior is to prove that we are not machines, an idea he got from Dostoyevsky. That's an interesting suggestion, but I'm not convinced. At least, I don't think that's the explanation for the episodes of procrastination that other people find most annoying. I can convince myself I am not a machine by doing things that will inconvenience me but not bother anyone else. I may leave for class so late that I have to run from my office to get to the classroom on time. I will arrive breathless but convinced that I am not a mere machine. That's not the sort of procrastination, however, that is most likely to get on the nerves of my wife or colleagues.

The sort of procrastination that others find irksome, I think, is usually a way of showing that you are not controlled by others. I am working in my study.

My wife pops in to remind me to check the Visa bill, on which she has, in her methodical way, noted some questionable items. She would clearly like me to stop what I am doing, remove my laptop from my lap, take the bill (which she is kindly holding in my face), and comply with her request forthwith—this in spite of the fact that there is no earthly reason to deal with the Visa bill today rather than tomorrow.

Probably I am not doing anything all that important. Perhaps I'm looking over the email from Harbor Supply, which consists of coupons for winches and solar generators and torque wrenches and the like. I have no use for such things, but I would like to be the sort of person who would have a use for them. Still, my wife does not know I am wasting my time (although she might suspect it). For all she really knows, I am halfway through writing a paragraph that, had she not interrupted, would have changed the course of the history of philosophy. So I am annoyed.

As a result I delay checking the Visa bill even longer than I ordinarily might have. The point is not to harm myself or prove that I am not a machine. The point, insofar as there is one, is to show her that interrupting her husband in the (possible) throes of creative thought doesn't really serve a purpose.

This is really very immature on my part and cannot be justified as an instance of productive structured procrastination. I am not putting off reviewing the Visa bill as a way of doing something else worth doing. Indeed, my wife is giving me a nice opportunity to put off even further whatever I was already putting off by going over the Harbor Supply coupons—making up my mind about next quarter's textbooks, perhaps.

The idea that by not checking the Visa bill immediately I will discourage my wife from such interruptions is quite absurd. The pattern in question has gone on for about fifty years.

My advice is: Don't confuse structured procrastination with providing proof to your spouse that he or she doesn't control you. Trying to prove something to your spouse by not doing things should be reserved for really unreasonable demands. Which, just for the record, my wife never makes.

Neil is particularly irritated by his procrastinating academic colleagues. He thinks that in their case the cause is probably academic arrogance, "the belief that ordinary rules do not apply to the great thinkers, even if flouting those rules results in harm to others." I'm sure he is right that some of his procrastinating colleagues are possessed of such arrogance. I'm pretty sure this is not the right diagnosis for the typical structured procrastinator, however. Most of us feel guilty when we miss deadlines. We are pretty commonly moved when we see that our procrastination is harming others. The truly arrogant academics don't see their procrastination as procrastination. They instead view it as a correct ordering of priorities that others simply don't appreciate: "Would they *really* have me grading papers this morning, when by rereading Kant's *Groundwork* I may be inspired to add another ten pages to the hundred thousand or so that have already been published on it?"

Structured procrastinators tend to be humbler sorts, who feel bad about inconveniencing others. For example, I have carefully determined exactly how far I can miss the deadline for reporting grades without inconveniencing my students. This gives me about an extra half-day. I take that as an absolute deadline, that absolutely cannot be missed, and as a result I don't miss it all that often. I think arrogant procrastinators and structured procrastinators are different subspecies.

And why is Neil so worried about the bookstore? If I have a colleague who is worried about my late book orders, I just might suspect that he or she was a bit of a busybody, and that might lead me to indulge in anticontrol procrastination of the type we considered above in relation to spouses. That would be immature and unworthy, however.

Much better would be to directly confront the (possible) busybody with some good philosophical advice. After I posted Neil's email on my webpage, another reader came up with this in response:

Why do people sometimes not use the crosswalks? And why when they say the party is at 7:00, does no one show up until 8:00? And why is it that most people drive over the "maximum" speed limit? Why do girls say they like nice guys, but they never date them? Why do people say one thing and do another? Why can't everybody just follow the ordinary rules?

Zoom out some. It will all be over soon enough. Sun go boom.

—Jim Stone

CHAPTER TEN

Deep Concluding Thoughts

Man is a rational animal. —**ARISTOTLE**

Man is not a rational animal,
he is a rationalizing animal. —**ROBERT HEINLEIN**

Man is a rational animal who always loses his temper
when he is called upon to act in accordance with
the dictates of reason. —**OSCAR WILDE**

It has been said that man is a rational animal.
All my life I have been searching for evidence which
could support this. —**BERTRAND RUSSELL**

Aristotle thought man was a rational animal. We certainly have the capacity to think, reason, deliberate, and act on the basis of our reasoning and thinking. We seem to have this capacity to a larger extent than do most other animals, although I'm sure we exaggerate the difference and probably also exaggerate the advantages it confers on us as a species.

But whatever we are, we aren't simply rational decision-making machines. We are basically bundles of desires, beliefs, urges, and whims. At any given time, a number of desires of various sorts are competing for control of our bodies and thought processes. The dutiful me wants my body to get out of bed. The comfort-loving me wants to turn over and sleep for another few minutes—or couple of hours, perhaps. The rational me wants to answer my email in the order it arrives. The curious me, however, wants to look at the new stuff to see if there is anything titillating there, to search for opportunities to waste time and stave off useful work as long as possible. Part of me wants to be healthy and fit; another part wants a cookie or a cigar.

Rationality is a wonderful gift, but for most of us it's no more than a thin veneer on top of our bundle of disparate desires, or perhaps it's just an additional desire, comparatively weak, that competes with the rest of them. For some the wish to be rational has become such a strong, dominant desire that it guides a great proportion of their action. I am thankful for such people. They accomplish a lot; they are wonderful, if tiring, to work with; much that is good about my life is due to their efforts. Of course, I am thinking of the ones who devote their energies to beneficent goals. Resoluteness and rationality in pursuit of evil is no virtue.

But the life of a structured procrastinator has much to recommend it. The great economist and political philosopher Friedrich Hayek used to emphasize that in the life of society, spontaneous organization is usually more productive than central planning. He had in mind developments such as human language and the market system. These were the results of human action but not the results of some human or committee of humans deliberately designing them. Like all great political philosophers, Hayek probably pushed his insight too far; if he didn't, his disciples surely do. But still it's an insight. A similar one holds for individuals. You may often be wrong about what the best way to spend your time is. Wasting your time daydreaming about an impractical radio show may in the end prove more valuable than finishing whatever articles, reviews, and memoranda—all doomed to be largely unread—you could have been working on. The structured procrastinator may not be the world's most effective human being, but by letting her ideas and energies wander spontaneously, she may accomplish all sorts of things that she would have missed out on by adhering to a more structured regimen. Pat yourself on the back for what you do get done. Use to-do lists, alarm clocks, and other ways of booby-trapping your environment. Form collaborations that will prevent you from never accomplishing anything. Above all, enjoy life.

APPENDIX

How to Kick the Habit—
Read at Your Own Risk

One of my primary goals for this book has been to make structured procrastinators feel better about themselves—rather than to turn them into nonprocrastinators. If I knew of a quick, easy, sure-fire way to cease procrastinating, I would have shared it, honest. I hope that, having read this book, you are feeling better about yourself and realize that you're managing to be productive in spite of procrastinating. In that case you may have more important things to do with your time and energy than try to rid yourself of this flaw. Perhaps you should close the book now.

But if you are not satisfied with being a structured procrastinator and want to become a nonprocrastinator, more power to you. I'd like to be helpful. I haven't read all the articles, blogs, and books that have been written to help procrastinators overcome their bad habit, but I've read lots of them and intended to read many more. Some have helped—but not many. Here are some pointers, toward some things and away from others.

Articles

The world is full of articles that are intended to frighten people out of procrastinating. One example is by Hara Marano, an editor of *Psychology Today*. Its subtitle is "Is Your Procrastination Hindering You? Ten Things You Should Know."[1] You might think the ten things are useful bits of advice. But no. The ten things turn out to be not-so-nice facts about yourself.

Some of these facts that Marano is so eager to impart I'm quite sure you already know—like that procrastinators distract themselves from things they ought to be doing. The new things will just make you

[1] By Hara Estroff Marano, published on August 23, 2003. http://www.psychologytoday.com/articles/200308/procrastination-ten-things-know.

feel worse about yourself. For example, procrastinators drink too much because of problems of self-regulation, and procrastination may compromise your immune system. Isn't that pleasant to learn? My advice: Avoid this article and others like it. They will simply provide you with semi-scholarly ammunition for describing various things you already know are wrong with you and raise fears about even worse problems you may have. Reading such articles will lead to anxiety and self-loathing but won't help you deal with your tendency to procrastinate.

Books

Much the same can be said for many of the self-help books dealing with procrastination. A lot of them begin by trying to motivate you to change by telling you how awful you are to be procrastinating in the first place. Then they go on, sometimes at great length, providing advice and exercises and other tools. The problem is that reading them, working through the exercises, and taking the advice is the sort of thing one could do only if one were not a procrastinator in the first place. The true procrastinator may start a long, boring book full of self-help exercises, but he won't get very far and instead will end up feeling more miserable than ever.

One exception is *The Procrastinator's Digest*, by Timothy Pychyl, who was one of the experts consulted in Marano's article. His book gets off to a good start, with Dr. Pychyl telling us that he assumes we are reading it as a way of avoiding something else we are supposed to be doing. That suggests some insight into his audience.

Dr. Pychyl reasons from that premise that he ought to keep the book short and lively so he won't lose his readers. He does a pretty good job at this. The chapters are brief. Each one starts with a mantra that you are supposed to say to yourself and write out on a sticky note to paste on your refrigerator. Some of these are quite good:

Feeling good now comes at a cost.

I won't feel more like doing it tomorrow.

Just get started.

They aren't all winners, however. For example, I don't find this one all that inspiring:

My personality provides both risk for and resilience against self-regulation failure.

If I pasted that on my refrigerator and my family saw it, I think they would begin to look at me oddly.

Nonetheless, if you can commit yourself to leaving procrastination behind, Dr. Pychyl's book will help you, I'm sure.

You might prefer a more indirect approach, however. If you want to stop procrastinating, it may be because you realize that procrastinating is making you unhappy. Perhaps you should go directly to the project of being happy and let procrastination take care of itself. If you want to know what happiness is, you need to go to the philosophers. Start with the Wikipedia article "Philosophy of Happiness." Then go to the

Stanford Online Encyclopedia of Philosophy, search for "happiness," and follow through the articles that come up to see what various philosophers have said. Then read the philosophers' works themselves. By the time you're done, you'll probably be dead, whether or not you are happy.

As I indicated in Chapter 8, "Fringe Benefits," it's a good idea to benefit from the work of gung-ho people. In the case of happiness, plenty of people have conducted their own search for happiness by reading all the relevant philosophical and psychological literature and reporting what they discovered.

One rather nice book is called *The Happiness Project*, by Gretchen Rubin. It records her experiences during the year she made a determined effort to find happiness, or at least to find more happiness than she already possessed. Now clearly Gretchen Rubin is no procrastinator. She belongs to a different species, one that I'd call enthusiastic accomplishers. It's up to the rest of us to benefit from all of her hard work. Along with the story of her search for contentment, her book is full of information about the psychology of happiness, explained in a very readable way. Both Pychyl and Rubin have websites, so if you like their books, you can go online to find out more.

Websites and Online Tools

Many colleges and universities have programs to help procrastinators get going. Much of the material is online, some of it quite helpful and much shorter than a typical self-help book. The University of North Carolina has a pretty good one: writingcenter.unc .edu/resources/handouts-demos/writing-the-paper/ procrastination.

It focuses on writing (avoiding term papers and the like) but explores more general applications as well.

There are lots of other online tools that might help you become less of a procrastinator. Google Calendar lets you set up reminders that nudge you at various intervals before a scheduled deadline or event. I'm sure other calendar programs offer similar options. This can be useful not only in reminding yourself of something